Forward Roll

Forward Roll

BY ANN AND CHARLES MORSE
PHOTOGRAPHS BY STUART BAY

EMC CORPORATION
ST. PAUL, MINNESOTA

Library of Congress Cataloging in Publication Data

Morse, Ann.
    Forward roll.

    (Their Just like you, just like me)
    SUMMARY: As a member of an athletic family, Jim wants to be good at something—and takes up gymnastics.
    [1. Gymnastics—Fiction]   I. Morse, Charles, joint author.
II. Bay, Stuart, illus. III. Title.
PZ7.M84582Fo   [E]   73-14698
ISBN 0-88436-033-4
ISBN 0-88436-034-2 (pbk.)

Copyright 1973 by EMC Corporation
All rights reserved. Published 1973

No part of this publication can be reproduced, stored in a retrieval system, or transmitted in any form or by any means; electronic, mechanical, photo copying, recording, or otherwise, without the permission of the publisher.

Published by EMC Corporation
180 East Sixth Street
St. Paul, Minnesota 55101
Printed in the United States of America
0987654321

JUST LIKE YOU, JUST LIKE ME
MAX-I-FISH
ON A TIGHT ROPE
LOST AND FOUND
FORWARD ROLL

U.S. 1991067

Jim Green wanted to be good at something. His sister, Donna, won three medals in swimming. His other sister, Molly, was on a soccer team. Even his friend, Benny, knew everything about football. And he knew everybody on all the teams. Jim wanted to be good at something. But he didn't like baseball or football or hockey. He wanted to be good at a sport he liked.

One day Jim's mother told him about some classes after school. Gymnastics. Cooking. Tennis. Jim asked about gymnastics. "Does that mean you do stuff in the gym?"

Jim and his mother read about gymnastics. "Come and learn what you can do. Learn to tumble. Learn to balance yourself. Learn to jump on a trampoline. Learn what your muscles can do. Come every Tuesday and Thursday at three o'clock in the school gym."

"That's it. That's what I want to do," Jim told his mother. She thought it was a good idea and made plans for Jim to go.

Jim told Donna and Molly about his new class. They both said, "Gymnastics? What's that?"

Jim rode his bike over to Benny's house. "Hey Benny, I'm going to take gymnastics," he shouted. Benny was tossing a football with his brother.

"Gym who?" Benny said. Benny kept on playing. "What are you going to do?" Benny asked Jim.

10

"I'm going to take gymnastics at the school gym. I will learn to do some things on the mats." Jim told Benny about the tumbling and the trampoline. "Want to join up for the class too?" Jim asked Benny.

"It might be fun. But I like football. Gymnastics doesn't sound like a real sport to me." Benny saw the smile go away from Jim's face. "I mean it will be lots of fun for you. I just don't want to go. I'm sorry, Jim."

"That's okay. Doesn't matter." Jim waved and rode away on his bike.

"I don't care," Jim said to himself on the way home. "I'm going to gymnastics. And I'm going to get good at it."

Tuesday came. Jim was glad that gymnastics would start that day. It seemed to take forever for school to be over. Three o'clock finally came. Jim had waited all day. Now he felt a little scared. "Why did I ever join up for this anyway?" he asked himself. Jim got a drink of water and it felt funny going down.

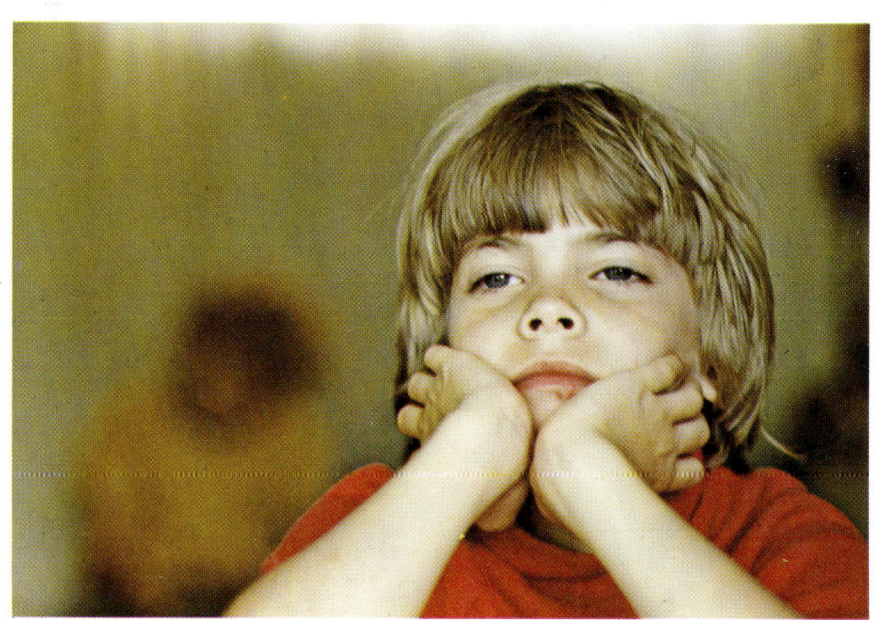

One, two, three, four, five, six. There were six other kids in the gym. Jim knew most of them. The gym teacher came in with another man. "Hi, kids," he said. "Everyone ready to start gymnastics class?"

"This is Lee Johnson. He will teach you gymnastics. Lee is a gymnast. He has won lots of medals. And Lee has been in many meets in the state. You can call him Lee."

Lee looked very strong. "He sure must know what to do with his muscles," Jim said to the girl beside him.

"Let's start by taking off our shoes and socks," Lee said. "We will start out in the warm-up sit. That means you sit with your legs straight out in front. Now do the straddle sit. Stretch your legs out to each side. Stretch your arms straight out. Touch your toes."

"This is easy," Jim thought.

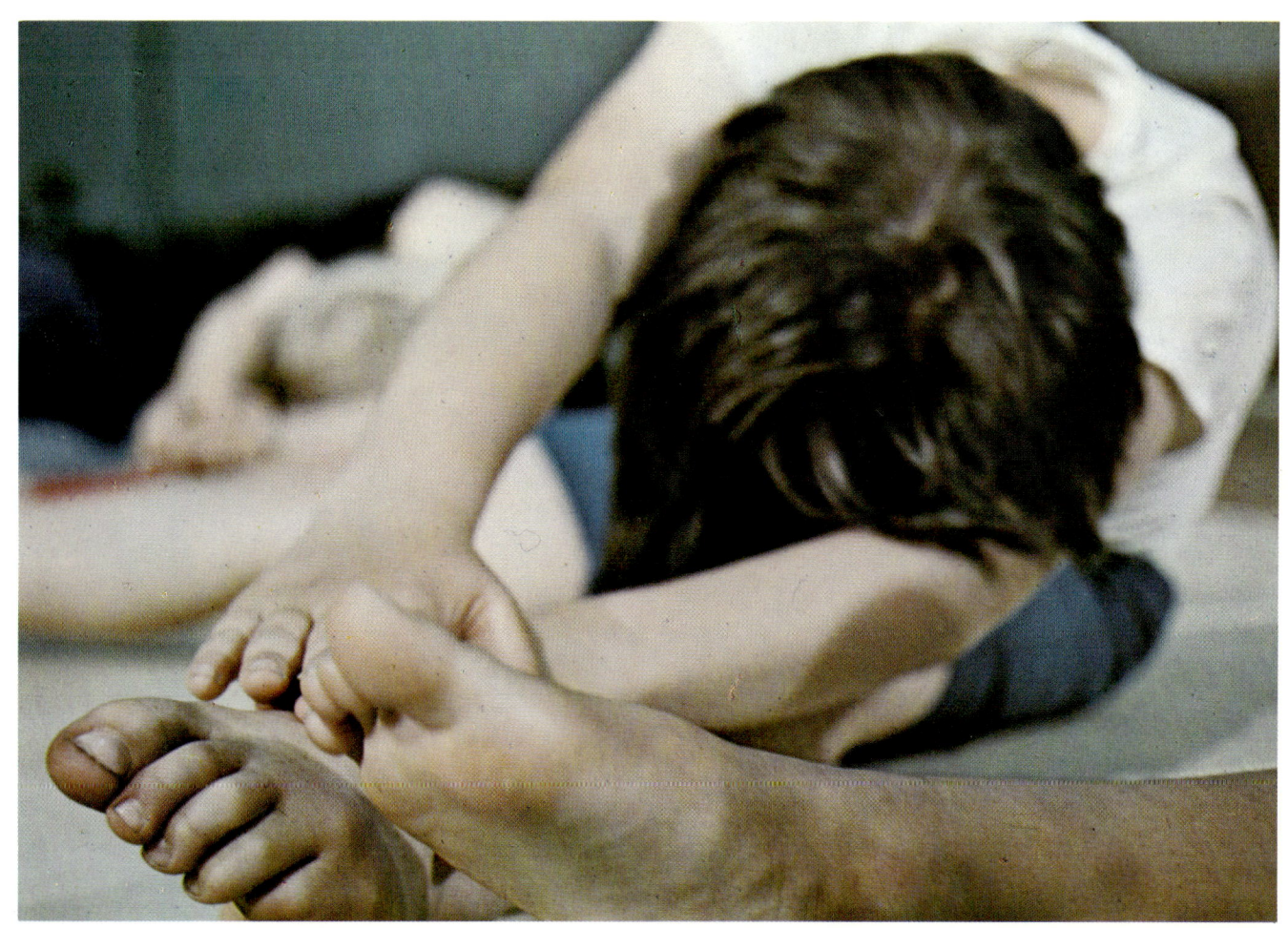

17

Lee kept on. "Stretch your arms out. Now do the 'V' sit. Make your body look like a 'V.' "

Jim felt his legs hurt. "A 'V' is hard to be," Jim said softly.

"We will work on being a 'V' again," Lee said. "Now let's make bridges. Lie on your back. Push with your hands. Lift your tummy up. Heads back. Good. There are many good bridges here."

That was fun. Jim felt as if he were a real bridge.

"Now a forward roll," Lee said. "You might call it a somersault. But we call it a roll in gymnastics."

"Oh, we know how to do that," everyone said. And they all tried a roll. But some went forward. Some went to the side. And some got stuck in the middle.

"Let me show you how to do a roll," Lee said. "Arms straight ahead. Tuck your head under. Roll and stand up with hands straight out."

22

Jim could roll over pretty well. But it was hard to stand up right away. And so the class went on. The children learned new ways to jump. Lee showed them new ways to kick their legs. They saw Lee do the splits. And they each got a turn to jump on the trampoline.

On the way home, Jim felt sore. Even the next day, Jim still felt sore. He hoped some of the hurts would go away before Thursday. Gymnastics was harder than he thought. But Jim didn't tell anyone how hard it was. He was afraid his family might laugh at him.

Each Tuesday and Thursday Jim tried hard to do the things Lee showed them. It was hard for Jim to put his hands on the mat and then kick his legs up. So he worked on it at home.

"You look funny," Benny said to him one day. Jim was working on kicking his legs up. He could stay up longer if he rested his legs against the side of the house. Jim could feel his face getting red. He wished Benny would go away.

"I have to work on my gymnastics, Ben," Jim said. He put his feet down and started to work on a backward roll. Benny kept watching. "I will never learn to do all these things," Jim said to himself.

U.S. 1991067

One day a new boy came to class. His name was Ronny. He didn't even know what a forward roll was. And Ronny had to watch when the kids did tuck jumps on the trampoline. It was a hard class for Ronny.

After the class, the teacher stopped to talk with Jim. "Jim, can I give you a job?" Lee asked.

"Sure," Jim said. He wondered what Lee would want him to do.

"I would like you to help Ronny. Can you help him at home? It is going to take him some time to catch up with you and others in the class. Can you help him?" Lee asked.

Jim didn't know what to say. "Do you think I'm good enough? I mean do you think I can really teach him something?" Jim felt good. It was nice to have Lee ask him to help Ronny.

So each day after school, Ronny came over to Jim's house. They both worked on bridges and on forward and backward rolls. They worked on jumping with knees bent and landing on their toes.

Jim showed Ronny how to kick his legs up and rest them against the house. He showed him how to turn cartwheels from the right side and from the left side.

It was a funny thing to help Ronny. Jim was learning something too. Jim didn't need to have someone tell him that he was getting good at gymnastics. He was beginning to see for himself that he was good at something.

30

At the next class, Ronny showed Lee how well he could do the straddle jump. Jim smiled. And Lee winked at Jim. Jim felt proud.